AF223829

Publisher: Cathy's Connection to Hope (CCTH)
                cathymcallister12345@gmail.com

First Publication, June 2022

ISBN 978-168524421-7

Printed in United States of America
by Ingram Sparks www.ingramsparks.com

All Bible references from the New American Bible, authorized by United States Conference of Catholic Bishops, World Bible Publishers, Inc. revised edition, 1987

Editor: Lacey Freiburger AAS,CMA(AAMA)
Graphic Design: Amy Flores

DANCING WITH THE MOST HOLY TRINITY: GOD ADVENTURES
MINI BOOK 2

BY

CATHY MCALLISTER, OFS

Cathy's Connection to Hope
cathymcallister12345@gmail.com

CONTENTS

DEDICATION

To all God's children. That means you, the
READERS, me, and every other human being

To all God's creation "...respect all creatures, animate
and inanimate" (Rule 18 of Secular Franciscans)

THANK YOU TO:

TO GOD THE FATHER WHO CREATED ME

TO GOD THE SON WHO SUSTAINS ME

TO GOD THE HOLY SPIRIT WHO INSPIRES AND GUIDES ME

Father Fey, my Spiritual Director when I was a teenager

Readers who motivate me and provide feedback to enrich future writings

Contributors of their God Adventures

FORWARD
MINI BOOK 2

THE REASON FOR SHARING MY STORIES
Cathy McAllister, OFS

Paul's teaching in his letter to the Corinthians begins, "The grace of our Lord Jesus Christ and the love of God and the fellowship of the Holy Spirit be with you all." Grace and the gift of the Trinity are given by the Father through the Son in the Holy Spirit. Showing care, concern and kindness to others, whether we belong to a church, profess a faith or not, God the Father unconditionally loves each person. The Son provides grace and strength. The Holy Spirit moves and inspires action.

Life is a journey. It is a circle from God back to God. St. Thomas Aquinas describes it as "the Great Circle of Being," … a kind of circular movement, in which all things return, as to their end, back to the very place from which they had their origin in the first place." <u>Book of the Sentences</u>, I dist. 14, q.2, a.2 (The '<u>One Thing' in Three</u>, Father Michael Gaitely, Pg. 58) When considering the concept of "hindsight" one can see how our adventures create this circle. Another phrase is "what goes around comes around"; this is part of dancing with the Most Holy Trinity. We are created with free will and make our choices. The goal is that we will return to our Creator. As a child, I learned the question in the <u>Baltimore Catechism</u>, "Why did God make you?" The answer is, "God made me to know Him, to love Him, and to serve Him in this world, and to be happy with Him forever in the next." (Bishop Spalding, copyright 1985, Baltimore Catechism Number 1)

In the <u>Theology of the Body</u> by St. Pope John Paul II, he talks about marriage love between people. He further explains this kind of love is also applied to our marriage with God.

Unconditional love naturally goes out to His children. We spread it to others through the dance, thus boomeranging back to each of us. Let's take our cue from the following song.

> **"Dance, then, wherever you may be,**
> **I am the Lord of the Dance said he,**
> **And I'll lead you all, wherever you may be.**
> **And I'll lead you all in the Dance, said he".**
> ("Lord of the Dance", Dubliners, 1975)

Continue with me through my and others God Adventures, included in this mini book 2. Our Creator loves us and basks in joy, as He watches us go through the dance of life. He is ready to sweep us up and carry us over the mud puddles and through floods of life to safety and warmth.

PART 1

MAJOR STORY

Blessed with Three Vocations

BLESSED WITH THREE VOCATIONS!
RIDING THE "BICYCLE BUILT FOR TWO"

**For I know well the plans I have in mind for you, plans for welfare and not for woe, to give you a future of hope."
– Ezekiel 29:11**

Child – God's Work as a Teen - Convent – Single – Married – Annulment -Single – Married – Annulment -Single – Married – Secular Franciscan - Widowed – Single – Dedicated to God's Work

PART I BEGINNINGS OF GOD ADVENTURES

As I pondered, I realized my first remembered God Adventure was the death of my dad. I was very close to him. He was funny, laughed and enjoyed life. I especially remember sitting in the bathroom watching him shave, and being taught how and singing "Home, Home on the Range". My dad's favorite TV shows were Perry Mason, Gunsmoke, Jimmy Durante, Red Skelton and The Honeymooners.

In 1959, I was in 7th grade at St. Ann's grade school in San Antonio, Texas. We had only been there about one and a half years, after moving from Illinois. My class was studying about death, heaven and hell. One night in November, the priest was called to the house to give my dad the last rites, Extreme Unction. (It is now called Anointing of the Sick.) He had another heart attack. We used the sick call crucifix that had candles and holy water inside. Next, he was taken to the hospital. It was the last time I saw my dad alive, as children were not allowed to go to the hospital in the '50s. My brother was 9, I was 12 and my sister was 13.

After two weeks, my dad died. I remember telling God that I understood if he needed my dad back it was ok. I had such a gift of faith that I was consoled. We had to take dad back to

Illinois on the train for burial in his little home town of Hume. No funeral home in this small town meant my dad was laid out in my grandmother's living room. The priest said a rosary of seven decades when there is usually only five decades. Years later, I found out a seven-decade rosary is the Franciscan Crown Rosary, as I am now a Secular Franciscan!

I did not cry during this entire time from sick bed to prayer before the day of funeral, funeral Mass and burial. I wondered what people thought of me because I wasn't crying, but I also knew it was God's plan. I missed him a lot; he was my support if I had problems. Now God, became my support as can be seen and understood through my other Adventures. This adventure with God included faith, love and support of my siblings and helping our mom, as she went from work to hospital to home on a bus. We took Dad back to Hume on the train. Upon arriving, we were back on the farm with relatives, with whom we started our first ten years of life. Support came from our Catholic prayers and so many family and community members.

The adventure which began in 1959, did not come to fruition until around 1995. It was at a family reunion back in Hume, IL. We gathered with our entire family, mom, sister, brother, their families and mine, as well as, half sister and her children. I think only one nephew or niece was missing. We ventured to the cemetery in Marshall, IL and located his grave. He was buried next to his first wife, and daughter who had died in a car fire in the 1940's. While gathered at the grave site, I finally CRIED, with JOY as I felt this gathering was a GIFT FROM GOD as a favor for my dad!!!!

UNDERSTANDING: that there is often fruit from loss that doesn't show itself for a long time; do not give up and KNOW that God has the plan

BLESSED WITH THREE VOCATIONS!
RIDING THE "BICYCLE BUILT FOR TWO"

PART 2 - LEGION OF MARY AND SODALITY: WORKING FOR GOD

"Grant that we may all seek to serve our neighbor, by doing good and building up the community of love." <u>Liturgy of Hours</u>, 7th Week of Easter, Wednesday, Intercessions, Pg.186

Through this journey of vocations, God prepared me by what my mom taught by example: perseverance, find a solution to any problem and my CATHOLIC FAITH. I ECHO LOUD AND CLEAR what my sister said, that our Catholicism was the best gift Mom and Dad gave us. My guides were my Spiritual Director, Father Fey, my mom and Emily Read. Emily was a Third Order Secular Franciscan, the lady I attribute to my strong desire and love of serving God and His people. My formation began at age 12 as a member of the Legion of Mary and the Sodality.

Ah, what a glorious and blessed childhood I had when I was finally allowed to join the Legion of Mary and Sodality of the Blessed Virgin Mary. This was at age 13, summer before my 8th grade at St. Ann School. My sister already belonged. We met with Emily Read, and ten other girls, and boys on Monday nights. I still pray the Legion of Mary prayer brochure. It includes the rosary and Magnificat. There would be singing of Marian hymns. Afterwards Emily would pile us into her tiny Volkswagon and off to the Dairy Queen for a small sundae. This was in 1960.

As part of this group, our apostolate was varied. On the first Saturday of the month, Emily, Patricia, and I would meet Father O'Callaghan at two local nursing homes. Our job was to hold the candles as Father went from room to room distributing communion. My sister, at age 75, continues to do this apostolate at a medical center and a Skilled Nursing Facility in CA. She utilizes her Spanish which is such a gift and blessing.

There were two Nursing Homes within 10 blocks of our home to which we would visit weekly. I was so naïve that I went home and told mom that the Nursing Home took a lady's clothes away and wouldn't let her leave. Mom eased my mind and, of course, now I understand the dynamics!

Another lady was named Cathy, spelled just like my name. My affinity toward her grew; even though she never talked to me, I would talk to her and she would listen. A third resident taught me how to make a smock style pillow. There were so many different people, and so many lessons learned, having fun serving God.

Other God adventures included the following: One Sunday a month, our group would go to downtown San Antonio, and pray the rosary over the radio. Several of our Legion of Mary group, became Candy Strippers and visited the children at Santa Rosa Hospital. During the summer, from 1960 -1963, we went to the west side of San Antonio to teach migrant children. They missed many days of school because of their migrant work, therefore, our goal was to help them become ready for the next school year. I also had a chance to practice my rudimentary Spanish. (Little did I know that in the 1970's I would work full time in Michigan for United Migrants for Opportunity! Of course, God knew!!)

On weekdays I would rush home from the school bus stop, 12 blocks away from home, to be picked up by Emily. We would go to 5:30 PM Mass and lead the rosary before Mass. Once, I was late and missed my ride to church. It was too far and not enough time to walk to church. I sobbed a lot, because I wouldn't be able to receive Jesus in Holy Communion. Now I know about the Spiritual Communion prayer if I cannot go to Mass. Amazing!

Sunday mornings were FANTASTIC!! And, now again at age 74, I find myself serving God four hours on Sunday mornings. Back in the '60's I would go to 9:30 AM Mass, cook breakfast for the priests, answer rectory phones, and count children's envelope money. Then I would join Mom for Noon Mass. Now I am sacristan and have the privilege of setting up for 10 AM Mass. I arrive at 9 AM which gives me some quiet time before others arrive. I also serve as a Eucharist Minister and assist with noon Mass children's liturgy.

REALIZATIONS: Cutting my teeth on having such fun hanging out with God, His people and strong relationships. Astounding is a good word to describe the many "full circles" God has and is working in my life.

BLESSED WITH THREE VOCATIONS!
RIDING THE "BICYCLE BUILT FOR TWO"

PART 3 - CONVENT: GOD'S WISDOM

"You, Lord, control my destiny; the lot marked out for me is of the best. I will hold the Lord forever in my sight. With Him at my side I can never be shaken". Psalm16: 8

As I grew closer to the Lord and love in serving Him, a religious vocation was forming in my mind. My best girlfriend, Margaret, joined a convent right after 8th grade graduation. I was excited for her! My plan was also to join the convent, however, when and which religious order were the questions. My dad's sister was Aunt Sister Mary Blanche. She was a Dominican and Principal of Sacred Heart Academy in Springfield, IL. Sisters of Charity of the Incarnate Word were the sisters who taught me from fifth grade through sophomore year in high school. The Motherhouse was in San Antonio, Texas, my hometown.

Finally, after sophomore year, the papers signed, blessings from Father Fey and suitcase packed, I was realizing my dream, being a Bride of Christ! The first year, I was an aspirant and completed high school. Holidays and summer were spent at home. I was so proud to wear the black and white clothes with white starched cuffs. The second year, as a postulant, I attended Incarnate Word College as a freshman. The Motherhouse was at the top of the hill and the College at the bottom. There were no visits home, however, family could visit two times a year for two hours. Days included up early, morning prayers in chapel, chores, breakfast and lunch in silence, schoolwork, classes, additional chores and two-hour recreation and homework. The only time we talked was at supper and night recreation along with two hours on Thursday afternoon. Both years, I spent a week in bed from exhaustion. Another medical problem was that I was on a pre-ulcer diet and needed a glass of milk mid mornings. The rigorous regimen did not go well with my bodily system.

If this was an autobiography, I would have so many stories to relate. It would provide a great deal of humor. They were the two happiest years of my life. I loved being in the convent but May, 1965 it came to an end. I was called into the office, and it was suggested that I leave to "get my stomach in order." Going with my life philosophy, I adhered to "God's will". In 2016 it would have been my 50th year as a Bride of Christ, if that had been God's plan. It was nostalgic and, at times, tearful. It was a sacrifice that I willingly made.

WHAT DO I TAKE FROM THIS ADVENTURE? God's love, without doubt. It was an adventure that was filled with prayer, hard work, community, friendship, love, laughter and so many memories. Once again, just like my dad's death, I had no question God had the plan! Laughing, I tell God Thank You as He knew I did not want to be a teacher or nurse, as this is the work the sisters performed.

VIRTUES INCREASED: Trust, joy, patience, acceptance, flexibility, humility

BLESSED WITH THREE VOCATIONS!
Riding the "BICYCLE BUILT FOR TWO"

PART 4 - VOCATION OF MARRIAGE

**"I've been cheated, been mistreated. When will I find love?"
(Linda Ronstadt, 1974)**

These words were being played while enjoying a stretching and toning water class. It brought back memories of sitting in the bathroom crying during my second marriage. It is a very clear image of crying out, "God, I have so much love to give but no husband wanting it."

These God adventures have many heartaches, troubles, challenges, sadness, loneliness, etc. I know I never doubted God's love, but as a human and as a wife, love, kindness, caring, comfort and security was not present in my first two marriages. Oh yes, two marriages, annulments and widowhood. I had more years as a single mom than a married mom and woman!

"But I also see griefs that are evil at war in me with joys that are good, and I do not know which will win the day. This is agony, Lord, have pity on me! It is agony! See, I do not hide my wounds; you are the physician and I am sick; you are merciful, I am in need of mercy." "Confession of St. Augustine", Liturgy of the Hours, Wednesday, 8th Week of Ordinary Time, Pg. 274. St. Augustine's words say it better than I could.

Readers who remember back to the '50's and 60's TV shows saw the "perfect marriage" depicted. The woman was home taking care of family, husband and household. There was a husband who was kind, affectionate, sharing thoughts and earned a living to take care of the family's needs. My reality is that I earned the living, solved the problems, cared for the family while working and going to school full time, as married and as a single mom. Through my Catholic teachings I knew anger, intense anger, ferocious, had to be let go. I journaled my conversations with God. I cried; I begged for a happy "Holy Family" marriage.

It is imperative to remember that anger, especially if it turns to hatred, kills the one who is angry. It does nothing to the one or entity with whom we are angry. It creates a culture of death in all areas of life such as social, faith, physical and mental. The anger can build to hatred. Our body language will give it away to others. And, yes, people will worry about us.

Through years of soul searching, depression, journaling to God, retreats and counseling, I was finally able to acquire peace. PEACE is my most valued part of my life. If I or others, begin to see peace slipping away, I need to step back, stop and readjust. Prayer (talking to God) is always at the forefront of my recapturing peace back into my life.

My faith, trust and love of God allowed me to weather the storms, rain of tears and human aloneness. In 1967 thru 1990's saw a lot of physical and emotional pain, poverty and exhaustion. Also, in these adventures with God it also has RAINBOWS FROM THE RAIN!!! They include three wonderful sons, two fantastic daughter-in-laws, three grandchildren, friends, coworkers, other single moms, and tennis after work while kids played in the park, church family and many "miracles and blessings".

Deuteronomy 2:7 gave me hope and strength: "The Lord has blessed you in all that you have done; he has watched over your progress as you journeyed through the vast desert."

TEACHINGS: My God adventures taught me to be joyful, laugh, learn from life, victories over the devil, successes, patience, compassion, empathy, and lots of forgiveness.

BLESSED WITH THREE VOCATIONS! RIDING THE "BICYCLE BUILT FOR TWO"

Part 5 – WIDOWHOOD, SINGLE AND RELIGIOUS AS SECULAR FRANCISCAN

"For God never withholds good except when He has something better to give." Having a Mary Spirit, Joanna Weaver, Waterbrook Press, 2006, Pg. 3

Ever since Emily Read, our leader of Legion of Mary and Sodality, the Third Order of St. Francis lingered in my mind. She wore her Tau every day. This showed she was a Third Order Franciscan. I aspired to become one but never knew how to go about it. Lo and behold, it wasn't my time!! God knew and was waiting without me knowing a thing. When I moved from Lansing to Jackson, MI in 2001, I joined a new parish. That decision in itself was an adventure.

The first mailing I received was a list of organizations and activities in the parish. Oh, my goodness, Secular Franciscans were here!!! I made the call the next day to find out who I needed to speak with for more information. As I entered formation, a few months later I found out that Third Order Secular, which Emily was called, had been renamed Order of Secular Franciscans (OFS). Both the Poor Clare's and Seculars are Third Order. This change took place in 1978 by St. (Pope) John Paul II, the Great. The other "amazing" piece (as everything with God's timing is amazing), just a few miles from me in Lansing, was a Secular Fraternity at Holy Cross Parish. I lived in Lansing for 25 years. Another proof that God knows best!! Hind sight is enlightening. Those years in Lansing, I was definitely not ready to engulf myself in formation as a Franciscan!

Secular Franciscans come under the guidance and direction of the Pope. St. Francis of Assisi had to travel to Rome in the year 1221 and have the rule approved. Subsequently various Popes have given the approval of any changes made to the rule. Vows are not taken but rather evangelical counsels of obedience, poverty and humility are professed. St. Francis formulated his rule under the directives of Jesus' words to his apostles, to take nothing with them as they went about preaching and teaching the good news, accepting all people, professing love, and practicing poverty of spirit.

Seculars live within their own families, communities, parishes, workplaces, etc. We are able to meet people "where they are at". A Secular Franciscan (OFS) has a primary vocation as married, single, deacon or priest. We have a little red rule book that guides us in Franciscan way of life. My favorite is Rule 4, "Going from Gospel to Life and Life to Gospel". Justice, Peace, and Integrity of Creation is a major focus for OFS.

It took two and a half years of formation, before I was professed on February 4, 2004. Nedra was also professed at the same time by Father Jim Shaver (he is an ordained Diocesan priest but studied to be a Secular Franciscan too). My husband, Jim, was present and two years later he was also professed as an OFS. It was humorous because when I began my training the fraternity was so excited because "we have someone young"! I was 52 years old!!! A new formation minister was needed, and I was appointed. It was a privilege to assist in the formation of OFS' There were five in my first class, which included my husband, Jim. At this point, I am now the one saying, "Oh boy, someone young!" when we have new people Never a dull moment on one of God's Adventures!!!!

Labyrinth: a help to explore, ponder, listen to God, and discover insights and new ideas. It is a sacred space that can be used in one's own spirituality or belief system. Labyrinths have been used for thousands of years. "The God of Peace will soon crush under your feet. The grace of Our Lord Jesus Christ be with you." (Romans 16:20)

I have walked a labyrinth three times. On the first walk, I surprisingly found myself doing a life review of relationships. It ended up being a cleansing. I cried about the death of my father, being so young in life. Tears also came as I processed loss of my dream of being a nun/sister and having a "Holy Family" like Mary, Joseph and Jesus.

Another time, I walked a labyrinth it seemed like I was taking the same path I just walked. Then a realization came that even though there were two marriages ending in divorce and annulments, it was a different path. Lessons learned and tears shed were not the same. It also dawned on me that my adulthood only included 25 years of marriage and living with a husband. For fourteen years I was blessed with a wonderful soul mate in a platonic relationship before marrying him. We were able to live as man and wife for 8 years, ending in his death. I became a widow for the first time. For 26 years and counting my adulthood has been with a vocation as a single!!

REALIZATIONS: Now I can see the dance with the Trinity, fast, slow, dips, turns, and spins. As I have learned from many experiences, it is not good to know the whole plan as God knows. If I knew, I might be tempted to back away. All I need to know is what and when God chooses to divulge the information.

TO THE READER: **PONDER:**
• What vocations or way of life has/is been in your adventures?
• Describe reactions to changes, twists, turns, circles, ups and
  downs.

____

____

____

____

____

____

____

PART 2

HAVING FUN WITH JESUS
AKA
PERFECT JOY OF ST. FRANCIS OF ASSISSI

WHAT IS PERFECT JOY?
When life events seem to be going all wrong, frustrating, confusing, worry, agony, anger, fear and anxiety, we then LAUGH. What could have become despair, hopelessness and deep depression become SHOUTS OF VICTORY. "When we are weak but You are strong..." (2 Corinthians 13: 9) God's graces create surprising strength; therefore, when I am weak, I become strong. Tears and sobs became LAUGHS OF JOY!

TREATS FROM GOD

"Give and it shall be given unto you." LK 6:38

5/23/2018

<u>Devil:</u> "Stay comfortable and type your stories. You are typing stories about God. That is holy work. It is ok to not go to Mass and keep first idea of going to Lansing in the afternoon."

OR

<u>Me:</u> "Even though I am doing work to help bring God alive in ordinary life, I need the graces from Mass. God also deserves my attention and praising words. Get off the couch, get dressed and get going. Yes, that is the best thing to do!"

<u>Decision:</u> Which voice to follow?

And, WOW what a day. Treats galore from God!!! I ran into a lady I knew in my former parish when I lived in Lansing. Oh, it was so good to reconnect. She looks wonderful. Her daughter was one of my fellow travelers I mentioned in the Rome adventure (Mini Book 1). The couple sitting in front of me in church today were also people I knew 20 years ago in my Lansing parish. A few pews over was a fellow Secular Franciscan and prison minister so that was another wonderful surprise.

Then, after I picked up two boxes of books for my Thursday prison group from the Lansing Diocesan office, I finally returned a picture of Our Lady of Perpetual Help to the St. Mary's Cathedral Parish Office. This picture was given to one of the parolees I assisted in reintegrating into the community after prison life. Along with the picture, I wrote a thank you letter to the St. Vincent de Paul and Legion of Mary group who set up his entire apartment in the early 1990's. This was a long overdue activity. Thank You God!!!

Next, on the way home I was able to deliver a Keurig coffee maker to a lady from one of my support groups. The Holy Spirit reminded me it was the day I had set aside to purchase Dairy Queen gift cards as gifts for the nurses with whom I work. It is Nurses Week so instead of going home I detoured to Kroger. I really thought I bought four cards, $10 each. Well, lo and behold, SURPRISE, when I counted them after arriving back at my car, there were six for $15 each!!! LAUGH OUT LOUD. SQUEAL WITH DELIGHT. So, with DELIGHT, I gave one to a friend I ran into at the store because she does so much for others. Next, it was a quick stop to another friend to whom I occasionally visit for a quick hug and smile. Today she also received a Dairy Queen card. It was like God turned me into a Dairy Queen pixie! LOVE IT – SO MUCH FUN HANGING OUT WITH GOD!!!

LESSONS LEARNED: Do not pass up the Holy Spirit nudge because I might miss out on a whole lot of fun and good stuff; take the opportunity to be thankful; sharing God's gifts creates so much JOY!

TO THE READER: **PONDER:**
• What unexpected surprises have come in the last day, week, month, year?
• From whom or where did these experiences come?

TWO DAYS OF "WONDROUS DEEDS"
OF THE LORD

"Give thanks to the Lord, invoke his name, make known among the peoples His deeds"   Psalm 105, 1

Dear Reader, my prayer is that as you read the following, you will experience memories popping up that will be of "wondrous deeds" in you daily activities.

February 2, 2020

**I am teaching Children's Liturgy (CLOW) about Jesus being presented in Jerusalem's Temple. The night before I realized candles would be a good teaching tool to emphasize their "light" to others. I forgot to ask the church office about obtaining some. Upon entering the sacristy this morning at 9 AM, lo and behold, someone came in with two baskets full of small candles! "Thank You God", I prayed.

**I was not sure if I would have help with the CLOW for 10 AM Mass. From my many past experiences, I knew God would provide, if needed. As I was leading the children out of church who should be opening the door but my friend Denise. She is dynamite with the children. What a delight!

**It was a long morning and my body was aching considerably. At 9 AM I began as Sacristan, preparing the vessels for Mass, then leading CLOW for 10 and Noon Masses. I had not decided if I would stay for continuation of Noon Mass after CLOW as I was tired and hurting. Then, a fellow Franciscan told me Noon Mass was for our Fraternity's living and deceased fraternity members. That information made the decision; I would stay.

**Several people wanted to talk to me after Noon Mass. This delayed my returning the Children's Liturgy book to the sacristy. Another oops! was that my coat was locked in the Parish Center with car keys in the pocket. The result was needing to wait with

Marcia for her husband, Deacon Dave, and Father to finish their greeting of the congregation. She suggested we pray the rosary. I learned a new prayer after each Glory Be, "For the health and lives of unborn, pray for them".

**A huge gift from God was, in addition to getting the keys from my coat pocket, I ALSO FOUND MY LOST SET!! Voila! both sets restored! I saw them just laying on my coat as I put it in the car. This set I had lost 6 days earlier at the YMCA after swimming exercise. While I was praying the rosary with Marcia, I asked God to show me the keys when it was time; I was willing to wait. Again, Thank You, God. My guess is there are many "lost keys" stories!

**This was only the first five hours of February 2! The car needed gas. Because of unusual circumstances at Kroger, I had accrued $1 off each gallon of gas. I used .50 and what a blessing as my funds were quite meager. I ended the day with rest.

February 3, 2020 Feast of St. Blasé
** While saying my morning Liturgy of the Hours, the Holy Spirit reminded me that if I go to Noon Mass at St. Mary, Star of the Sea, the priest may be blessing throats. This usually happens on this feast day. By the time I arrived at church I forgot about the blessing being so grateful to God for nudging me to praise Him at noon. At the end of Mass, Father announced he would be blessings throat for anyone who wanted to receive it. Thank You, God.

After Mass was my Spiritual Direction appointment which reaffirmed the peace I have been experiencing. It also showed me how I have grown and was able to discern, with God's grace and guidance, how to "hold loosely" ministries in which I am involved. They may have served their purpose and may be time to "let go". Being able to talk to someone about spiritual matters which touch ordinary life is so important. It is right up there with heating, food, and gas for the car!

**The afternoon mail provided the remaining pieces of information needed for taxes. My appointment is for the next day.

THANK YOU, GOD FOR SO MANY BLESSINGS IN JUST TWO DAYS.

INSIGHTS: Importance of being flexible; understanding I do not need to know how life will work out but TRUST that it will; discard worry

TO THE READER: **PONDER:** daily activities and events jotting down the little blessings that have come your way. Some may be "little" to others but are really "BIG" to you. Don't forget to share with others and get their stories too.

____
____
____
____
____
____
____
____
____
____
____
____
____
____
____
____
____

PART 3

TRUST IN GOD

CHANGES: REVEALING AND DIFFICULT

"You, Lord, give light to my lamp, my God who lightens my darkness. With you I can break through any barrier, with my God I scale any wall." Psalm 18:29-30

In the Fall of 2011, I had an episode of depression, anxiety, and exhaustion. I am a clinical Social Worker and I kept denying the symptoms, especially exhaustion and crying ever so easily. At a doctor visit, he said, "I need you to go to the Emergency Room (ER"). I said, "I have patients to see at the clinic". This dialogue was repeated several times until I agreed to go to the ER. By the time the ER doctor came into the room I had a plan. "I think I need to go to the Partial Hospitalization Program." That is an intensive outpatient facility where I had worked part time from 1998 to 2000. Approval was obtained since I use to be a staff member.

I had no idea how badly I needed this treatment. At the time I was working at four outpatient clinics of the hospital, Radiation Oncology, Pulmonary and Cardiac Rehab and Diabetes. During this therapy I kept saying, "I can't go back there" over and over while crying and shaking. It took two weeks in this setting, 9 AM – 3 PM, several days a week, before I "graduated" and continued with weekly outpatient counseling. Since I was 65, I was blessed to be able to begin Social Security as well as receiving short term disability from work. This was important because my husband was not working. He was undergoing chemotherapy every two weeks, so my income carried us through this time.

When I returned to work in January 2012, my work duties changed from four to two clinics, instead of four, and work hours decreased from 40 to 30 per week. I maintained same benefits. See how God works things out. The clinic where I had the heaviest load, and was a catalyst for my mental breakdown, changed my daily hours so I only worked from 9 AM to 3:30 PM and no night clinics.   It was hard for me to give up some of my duties because I loved all the work. With humility and gratitude, this became a healthy compromise.

My husband continued his biweekly chemo all through 2011 and 2012. November 2012 he almost died from chemo, so it was stopped. He told the doctor he wanted God to oversee his future. The doctor complimented him on his strength and decision. Exactly one week later the cancer hit the brain. Hospice was started at home, however, at the end of one week, he was moved to Hospice House. Three weeks later, January 3, 2013, he died. I was now a widow.

I continued working. Early 2014 I was walking down the hall at the clinic and God said, "Time to retire". I said, "I thought the plan to retire was at 70". He said, "time to retire". I replied, "Ok" and felt lighthearted and a little excited. God knows best. I decided the date would be the second Friday in October, signed up for Medicare and Supplemental plan and gave my notice. This was around April. On the day I retired, while attending my last staff meeting, it was announced that the hospital would be closing this clinic in December of that year. God does know what is best!

A lovely retirement party was given for me. All my children were invited. Delicious homemade food was served. A beautiful homemade book about all the people with whom I worked, and a generous donation was gifted to me.

I then went on a wonderful train trip to Illinois visiting my farm cousins. Upon return I was able to maintain 12 hours a week at Radiation Oncology for another five years.

In November 2014, I took my four-day silent retreat with a group of six ladies. I was given the most fantastic room; it was called the "chapel room". The retreat was held in an old convent which was the residence of retired nuns. The window in this room opened right into the chapel. Seeing the tabernacle, I felt like I could reach out and touch Jesus. It was fantastic! I slept the nights with my window open; it was like sleeping in Jesus arms.

The first morning I woke up, I distinctly heard God say, "this is the year to take care of your body". I spent the next three days working with God, praying, listening, and meeting with my Spiritual Director, Lori. Needing to make changes, I spent a few days listing everything in which I was involved. There were 20 activities on this list, and all were long standing commitments. Part of this was work and part volunteer time.

In 2015, I started decreasing activities and I am still decreasing!! People say, "I thought you were retired." I answer, "I'm trying to get more retired."

My energy had been declining over the last several years. It has been noticeably decreasing for about nine months. My activity level had a max of four hours, then needing to rest for several hours. Next came new sources of pain and more episodes of exhaustion. Satan was trying to wear me down but REALLY GOOD NEWS. As a Catholic, I know the value of suffering for a Holy Purpose! The devil implanted thoughts of fear of doing too much because I will be down again. New pain in my left ring finger, unable to bend and a toothache which throbs and may be infected. Normal lower back pain and right knee, arthritis in left hand and arm, kicking it up a notch. The balance is still in progress. Crying from time to time could be a warning signal of depression.

And how does God help? Does He leave me struggling alone? No! He sent me help!!! An unexpected text came from my adoration prayer partner. She invited me to go to her church on Sunday to be prayed over by others. She was concerned because I had to cancel two adoration hours. I immediately accepted; her answer was "I look forward with great joy to learning what Our Lord is going to do for you." The devil did not give up and I almost cancelled, because I was unsure if I had the energy to travel 45 miles each way. I could not find anyone to drive me. Sunday morning, I gave the devil the boot, went and experienced peace on the way home!

Saturday afternoon. I bought an iced coffee for my neighbor/
friend/Holy Spirit messenger. We sat and I was able to weep and
talk about the pain and the exhaustion. This was not a pity party
but speaking out loud about the devil's trickery and negative
thoughts. BUBBLE BURST!! OFF WITH YOU SATAN!! I once again
AM WINNING THE BATTLE!

<u>THANK YOU   THANK YOU   THANK YOU GOD for Your trust in me.</u>

The next morning, I was sitting on my porch, saying my prayers,
listening to the traffic and birds. It was perfect peace and the
restoration I needed.

In June I went on a trip with my sister to visit with our cousins in
Illinois. We were gone ten days, slept late and, going to bed at
8:30 P.M. Most days, people would come to visit at Cousin Lois's.
Gallivanting around was minimal and only for a few hours at a
time. This was a true vacation.

**BLESSINGS AND GROWTH: peace, insight, joy, grace received
for strength, patient endurance, and victory**

TO THE READER: **PONDER:**
• What has been learned from difficult times in life?
• Who or what has helped during these times?

____

____

____

____

____

____

____

____

____

____

____

PRECIOUS GOLD

"But now, Lord, you are our Father. We are the clay, and you are our potter."   Isaiah 64:8

Gold is brought to my mind while observing Fall's changing leaves. This color, gold, also reminds me of the precious metal. Gold has impurities, just like all of us. In order to be purified, a VERY HOT fire is needed to cleanse the impurities. The gold also becomes more flexible. We are like the metal, hard and difficult to bend. The more heat taken from the "world" the more pliable one becomes. Heat can be turned up to different degrees. As we go through the furnace, we become strengthened. Here are some examples of "heat" which can cleanse the impurities.

- Prejudice
- False assumptions that one is unchangeable
- Lack of security and safety
- Lack of affection
- Sexual tensions
- Needing to be "right"
- Needing to be accepted
- Lonely
- Fearful
- Temptations of greed
- Anxiety
- Money worries
- Add others

God is the Potter. He knows how far and how long the heat is needed. Sometimes the fire goes down to a low simmer. There can be times of feeling empty, hopeless or numb. The Holy Spirit can blow gently on the embers until the fire springs to life again. It is important to know this is a normal process as simmering helps to blend the spices and elements of life as the gold circulates slowly through the body, mind and soul.

It is good to give one permission to be on "low", just "be" and rest for a while. Then, there are times when the heat is increased to the melting stage. This is the stage of "change", "conversion", or "metanoia". Your golden shape is changing.

Here is a partial list of what new shape may be created.
- A **CUP** to hold others sorrows or a blessing cup to share happiness
- A **TABLE** where people come to feast and rejoice, a place for reconciliation
- A **SPARKLING GEM** bringing sunlight and reflection to others. "He buoys up the spirit and brings a sparkle to the eye" (Sirach 34:17)
- A **GOLD COIN** that can be given to someone in need
- A **TRUMPET** to sing God's praises, bring life into another's emptiness, music to someone's soul, play taps to give witness to another's life and heralding someone back to God's eternal happiness
- A **CANDLE HOLDER** to light the darkness and help someone through the cave of despair
- A **GOLDEN CHARIOT** inviting and taking others into the Trinity's dance and adventure
- **GOLDEN SHOES** for walking and dancing solo or with others
- **GOLDEN WEIGHTS** to build strength enough to care for someone in need
- A **GOLDEN MICROPHONE** to loudly proclaim God's message to others and to read His Word
- A **GOLD CHAIN** which links people together offering greetings and hospitality, kindness and smiles.
- A **GOLDEN COMPUTER** which can educate, share, encourage and learn.
- A **GOLDEN VOICE** that can cheer, inspire and give praise

The "dance of change" happens when:
- we encounter people, places, and situations
- a decision needs to be made on which way to go, how to act or who to follow

- a need to stop and ponder the situation
- to decide if the music of the Holy Spirit is being drowned out by clanging, chaos, anger, or other voices

Here are three tools that may be helpful in making these changes.
- **PATIENCE** in waiting for God's timing for change.
- **HUMILITY** in being unconcerned about what people think or consequences to self. God's way and the world's way are different.
- **JOYFUL ACCEPTANCE** in finding the positive and leaving the negative behind.

Here is the thing. At first glance, The Holy Spirit's music and voice is not always happy, calm, easy or appealing. There are still mountains, hills, sludge, difficulties, straining, and being "out of my comfort zone." The Dance, however, ends in a peaceful comforting sense about self, a feeling of "this is right!" And on to the next Dance!

"I AM GOLD TO MY LORD"
"I AM PRECIOUS TO GOD AND OTHERS"
GO FOR THE ADVENTUROUS DANCE WITH THE TRINITY!!!

REALIZATIONS: I am more than "just ordinary"; I have purpose and talents; I can make a difference.

TO THE READER: **PONDER:**
Into what am I or have I been melted and formed?

____

____

____

____

____

____

____

____

PRECIOUS GOLD

PART 4

GOD ADVENTURES WITH INSPIRATIONAL PEOPLE

BLESSING IN THE SNOW

By Renee T

"When one finds a worthy wife her value is far beyond pearls. Her husband, entrusting her heart to her, has an unfailing prize." Proverbs 31:10-12

40 years of marriage ended in the death of my husband due to cancer. We had a lot of fun and interesting times. His name was Jim. He was a carpenter, designed cabinets and kitchen counters. In fact, our home in Harrison, Michigan was a product of his creativity. Situations he got us involved in were quite a variety: flea markets, heavy duty garage sales and a deli which featured fancy coffees, subs, soups and salads. I worked on these projects with him. We were a tight married couple. One of the things we shared was our love of classic cars. In our first years of marriage, I found him a special classic car, a '68 GTO, and he found me a special classic car, a '65 Mustang convertible.

Religion was not part of our lives as adults. He said, "It was jammed down my throat as a child". This meant he was against getting married in a church, however, he did approve of a DAV (Disabled American Veterans) Chaplain marrying us. I did not grow up in a family that involved church or God. The bottom line is that faith did not play an important part of our life together.

This brings me to think about a special part of his life which was being a Navy ship repairman in Viet Nam from 1969-1970. This was prior to our courtship. He was injured during his duty time and fought for veteran disability benefits. After many years it was approved. Jim realized this was going to be part of future care of me if anything happened to him.

Once during our marriage, I had an unforgettable experience in a church I visited. I was looking at a wall where there was an 8x10 oil painting of Jesus. The colors were so vibrant. All at once the church felt hot so I took off my coat; I saw Jesus standing behind

me. His arms were spread out. He said, "I shall not take him."
Then the church turned cold. I thought, "what just happened?" I
called my sister as she has been in this church before. She said
there was no picture on that particular wall. I think Jesus knew
how much I needed Jim.

Several years later Jim was diagnosed with cancer and went
through treatment for less than two years. In February, 2016 he
was becoming extremely sick and was hospitalized. February 13,
I brought him home from the VA hospital. February 14 he never
got out of bed again. I was there in case he needed anything
however I was not able to touch him due to his sensitivity to
pain. It was very hard to see this happening and Jim's struggle.
I didn't want to let him go but I felt helpless. Faith was coming
back into our lives through his sickness. While Jim was in the
hospital a friend of mine drew me to the VA chapel. We would
pray together. I needed her support and God's. While Jim lay
dying in our bed, I again kept praying for help. Early in the
morning of February 15, I called 911. It was hard, hard, hard
to know the paramedics were working on him in the bedroom
but, it was no use. At 5 AM Jim passed away. My sister and her
girlfriend came to help me and give the support I so needed. We
went back to her place that night. It was a cold and snowy night.

Several people came to visit and comfort me. When my
girlfriend was getting ready to leave the house, she went out the
door and yelled, "Oh my, you have to see this." In the new snow
fall was a design of two hearts, interconnected with one side
having a break. This was made by the tire tracks of two cars in
the parking lot. It seemed like the break made it so real that Jim
was truly gone from me on this earth.

Since this time, February, 2016, I have come to increase my
prayer life and meditation. I feel closer to God and sense more of
His Presence.

REALIZATIONS: appreciation of my husband; thankfulness of being able to be there for him in his last days; how amazing is our God

TO THE READER: **PONDER:**
Is there a blessing in the midst of pain and suffering that comes to mind? Share the story with someone.

GOD ADVENTURES WITH MOM

"O God You have taught me from my youth and to this very day I proclaim your marvelous works." Ps 71:17

I gave my Mom a "run for her money". Mom liked to use "phrases", and now I find myself doing the same. It is fun to try and figure out where they come from. Memories come back like "pick up your lower lip or you're going to trip on it." Yes, I do seem to remember pouting a lot, but I also think it did not get me far.

If I had known my favorite phrase, "God Adventures", life would have been much more fun. I might have found out I was a good person earlier than age 26! Now that my outlook on life is more spiritual, I can also see how I contributed to Evelyn becoming "Saint Evelyn Barrett". Once, I heard someone say we are either a saint or a saint maker! I have helped a lot of people become saints and I am only 74!!! More saints to come.

Back to Mom: Being 11 ½ months younger than my sister, Patricia, I thought I "should" be able to do whatever she did. NOPE!! Mom became my "mean" mom. Two times Patricia was allowed to go to Padre Island, and I had to stay home. Well, it really worked out good for me because she got horrible sun poisoning both times. See how God and Mom really looked after me!

Patricia was also permitted to join the Legion of Mary and Sodality a year earlier than I. I was so happy when I was finally allowed to go. Patricia and I did all kinds of God work together. It was a favorite time in life. (GO TO "<u>BLESSED WITH THREE VOCATIONS, Part II</u>" for more on this topic.)

A cherished memory with Mom is going with her to noon Mass on Sunday. I had already been at church for 9:30 Mass and helping at the rectory until noon. Another special time was occasionally on Saturday, our weekly cleaning day, Mom, and I ate PB and J sandwiches while watching "Twilight Zone" at four in the afternoon. Sometimes, before McDonald's was created, Mom would surprise us giving money to my sister to go buy $.25 hamburgers, and $.15 fries. My sister could drive so off we went to bring back food for all four of us (I have a brother too). What a treat!!! God was, and had been, continuing to teach us about "treats", rare and special, as well as, how to do with what is available with appreciation.

God, through Mom, taught us the necessary foundation to survive and thrive with joy, no matter what life thrusts in our way. It was the simple and, small, happenings that made life so rich. It took me until I was studying for my master's in social work to be able to compliment her on parenting. I was around 46 when I picked up the phone and called her to say I think she was a good mom. She was a single, hardworking, thrifty, Godly person.

My sister got it right when she said Mom's best gift to us was our faith. Mom made sure we went to St. Ann's Catholic school and then Incarnate Word High School. Money had to have been very tight, but we graduated and, to this day, continue to serve God. My brother went to St. Ann's, he was an altar boy and graduated in the first class from St. Anthony High School.

THANK YOU MOM   THANK YOU GOD
THANK YOU FOR THE LIFE-GIVING ADVENTURES

LESSONS LEARNED: Life is not always as bad as it seems; God's words, "For I know the plans for you." Jeremiah 29:11; do not wait to express appreciation to someone and for something

TO THE READER: **PONDER:**
• Think about times when "life wasn't as bad as I thought" or "wow, I did survive".
• Who or what deserves a thank you?

____

____

MEETING MARY

By Elena Flores-Whitinger
(Granddaughter of Cathy McAllister)

"The gift of counsel endows the soul with supernatural prudence, enabling it to judge promptly and rightly what must be done, especially in difficult circumstances."
Holy Spirit Novena, Day 7

On the afternoon of February 23rd, 2019, my best friend, Lindsey, and I encountered Mary, Mother of God. We were on a retreat with some of the college students at our local parish. The retreat was held at a beautiful camp building that was positioned next to a lake and surrounded by trees. There are a few nature trails on the property; one of which holds the spot in which we encountered our Mother.

During a break between lectures, Lindsey and I decided to take a walk. It was a snowy day, but warm for February. The trail paths were covered with snow and ice and almost none of the ground showed through. As we walked, we chatted about the retreat, life, and everything in between. At one point during the walk my vision started to blur, just ever so slightly, as if I had entered a cloud of smoke; however, there was no smell of smoke nor was there anything around us that could produce smoke. Feeling that it was an unimportant sensation, I said nothing to Lindsey and kept walking. But seconds later, something told me to talk to her about it.

So, I said "Lindsey, this is weird, but my vision is blurry…"

She surprised me when she answered, "so is mine…maybe it's because we are both tired. Let's keep walking and I'm sure it will go away."

We kept walking and our vision immediately returned to normal. A few seconds later, once again something told me to talk to

Lindsey. So, I asked her if we should go back to the spot where our vision had blurred, and she agreed that we should.

"I remember where the spot is, I noticed there was small patch of green moss showing through the ice," she said as we turned around. We walked back to that spot and, surely enough, our vision blurred in the same way. For a second time we decided to shrug it off and try walking again. However, after walking for a few seconds I said to Lindsey: "Do you think we should go back to that spot and pray there?" To which she replied, "I was thinking the same thing!"

We searched for the small piece of moss and once we found it, we closed our eyes and prayed for each other and for whatever needed to be blessed in that spot. When we ended the prayer and opened our eyes, our vision had completely returned to normal. We were amazed…and a bit confused. We decided to continue our walk back to the building where we had started. That is when a miraculous thing happened! As we walked, Lindsey mentioned that she started to notice that everything was suddenly tinted blue. Not just the sky, but also the trees, the buildings, the snow, and the ice on the ground. When she told me, I told her that I saw that same tint of blue in the air. We were once again amazed…and confused. When we finally reached the retreat center building, we told everyone about our experience. We wanted to know if there was anything significant about this spot or the strange blue tint we were seeing. One of the missionaries told us that the blue tint may be a sign that Mary was present, since blue is one of the colors, she uses to represent herself. It is also called a Marian Color. The priest confirmed that indeed, it was probable that Mary was trying to reach us. We were AMAZED and so glad to have gone through the experience together, otherwise we may not have listened to Mary's call to pray.

TO THE READER: **PONDER:**
• Where in your life can you slow down to notice the small
  miracles?
• How has a saint touched your life?
• Have you ever had a similar event happen to you?

PART 5

VICTORIOUS OVER THE EVIL ONE
=
PEACEFUL LIFE

VICTORY OVER PHYSICAL CHALLENGES

"We are afflicted in every way, but we are not crushed; full of doubts, we never despair. We are persecuted, but never abandoned, we are struck down but never destroyed.
2 Corinthians 4:8-10

In late July 2018, my son, Paul, drove us on a four-and-a-half-hour trip to Indian River, Michigan. We hooked up with my other sons, their wives, and the grandchildren. The first night we spent at a motel, which was pleasant and leisurely. I went to bed early. The next morning, Friday, we ate a delicious breakfast then on to the lodge. I only carried in a couple bags. Then WHAMO!! That was it, down all day Friday and Saturday. I was in bed more than up. The short time I was active, I was dizzy, sweating, nauseated and crying due to the overwhelming tiredness. I told my children, and all concerned, that this is part of God's plan to slow me down. They replied they understood my connection to God, but seriously doubted He wanted me to be so incapacitated! I listened and was at peace with what I was hearing.

Continuation of health problems reached a crescendo on Sunday, August 5th. As a rule, on Sunday, I give four hours of activity to God as a sacristan, Eucharistic Minister (EM) and assist with Children's Liturgy. This Sunday, upon arriving at the Sacristy, I experienced weak and shaky limbs, sweating, labored breathing, and nausea. It was necessary to sit down several times while preparing for 10 AM Mass. I finally said, "Yes God, I will go to the Emergency Room (ER) as soon as Mass is finished". I sat on the chair in the sacristy, feeling weak all over. As people came in to sign up for Lector and EM, I began to cry silently. It was necessary to ask someone to sub for me as EM and leader of Children's Liturgy. The deacon came over and prayed with me then I proceeded to a church pew.

When time came for children's liturgy, I felt slightly better, so I assisted the teacher. Upon returning to my pew, I began sweating even more and had a pain across the back. I knew these are classic signs of women having a heart attack. I now prayed to God to at least let me receive communion. After communion, I looked over at friends of mine, Dan and Denise. I knew they would be upset with me if I drove myself to the emergency room. As soon as Mass was over, they took me and stayed until it was decided I would be admitted for more tests.

I spent three days in the hospital. There were many tests. Bottom line is my heart is great and arteries are "whistle clean" according to the doctor. Regarding what was the reason I was so sick, it is still a mystery at this point. When asked, "What was wrong", I say, "We have to wait until the Holy Spirit discloses the plan to the doctors and all of us".

New revelation came in my need to ask for help. At one point during my hospital stay, I started crying, as I told my children this was the first time in my adult life, I ever remembered people staying with me in the hospital, altering their schedules as needed. I have had quite a few surgeries and, mostly, went by myself. Part of this was "assuming" my children would be too busy so I did not ask them for help. My friend, Nellie, strongly directed me to not leave my children out. I told them and they came.

The first morning back home I slept about 14 hours. It was much needed but then I became so overwhelmed, thinking about all the people I needed to keep updated on my situation, that I sat down and cried. I needed help!! I called my friend Carol. She came over and was my secretary. It was such a relief!! This God Adventure increased my awareness as to how many friends, family, neighbors, coworkers, and church people etc. with whom I am blessed. Thank You God, thank You God, thank You God!

My son took me to see my primary doctor on the hospital follow up. She continued to try and figure out how to help. During the appointment, she looked at Paul, saying, "she is so stubborn," meaning me. He smiled and I sheepishly said, "I don't understand why people say I am stubborn". We all laughed. The good news is I was given a referral to the lymphedema clinic and endocrinology clinic with a doctor I worked with for 14 years. I also ended up being off work and activities for six weeks.

Rightly so, my sister encouraged me to give up sacristan and Eucharistic ministries for a few months until we find out what is going on and how much I can handle. The next day, I emailed Andy and told him to take me off the lists for a while. He answered back, "we are all praying for you", which brought tears to my eyes with overwhelming love with which I am blessed. Tears were also because, I love to serve God and love being Sacristan, a Eucharistic minister and helping with children's liturgy during Mass. I have learned over the years the importance of sharing graces. Others will do what I did, and I will not be a hog of these graces. I will pay attention to God, and His messengers to keep taking care of my body.

More challenges popped up one week later, still August 2018. Red spots and pain appeared on the back, left side. Could it be shingles? Could this be the reasons for my body's drain of energy? The doctor's office gave me an immediate appointment. Yes, shingles, a mild case as I already have had the vaccine. It was not the reason for all my other issues.

"Oh God", I said, "here we go!" Perfect Joy is my salvation in dealing with all these changes and issues. More calls were needed to cancel more plans. My prison group and I were working on the "33 Days to Morning Glory" program, which would end in a consecration to Jesus thru Mary. Meeting with my brothers in prison must be put on hold for now, however, that will not stop their preparation for consecration, with, for and thru Mary to Jesus. The Devil hates this. Yes, hate is not too strong a word!!

The Holy Spirit gave me ideas on how to make these changes in a positive manner. My manager called, and I was able to give her possible places to obtain a temporary Social Worker, and how to notify the support group I facilitate about canceling a few meeting dates. My son, called to remind me I can order food online while laid up. Barb is presenting the Stephen Ministry Program to the Parish Council. For the Secular Franciscan picnic next Sunday, I had already prepared early, and the items can be picked up. Now, I have time to focus on God, as well as, "get more retired". As I write this story, music by John Michael Talbot is playing in the background creating a peaceful atmosphere. GOD AND LIFE ARE GOOD!

The next BIG BLESSING was subbing for the gentleman who usually conducts the communion service at the prison on Mondays. I wanted to give him time with his family as it was Labor Day. The men had the spiritual communion prayer printed on the board as they were not expecting anyone to come into the prison that night. Oh, they were so happy that Jesus was brought in for them! We had not seen each other for four weeks and so it was a big blessing for me as well. I was very weak and drained by the end of the hour. The men were so solicitous, asking if I wanted a wheelchair. I declined, resting as we prayed the rosary for the last half hour. All was good.

Next came the Holy Spirit Novena that I said as a thank you for the service our Stephen Ministers have provided during the first two years of our ministry. Whenever I say this novena I watch out for "fallout" from the Holy Spirit. It is usually a couple of weeks of being busy with the Holy Spirit's work which is given to me. I was showered with so many blessings.
a.   God's grace to adhere to my stringent diet plan to regain health from the trunk lymphedema with which I was diagnosed
b.   increase in energy with this treatment
c.   being able to do more around house, but only in 15-20 increments with rest between sessions
d.   lost one lady doing my housework but gained another one and obtaining equality in talent and delightfulness, willing to do "projects".
e.   return to work after six weeks, starting with only a few hours

per week, building back to 10-12 hours per week.

f.   in the comfort of my living room, attended my first Webinar, Catholic Writer's Guild Conference, Friday – Sunday, learning so much to help me in writing this book.

g.   hired a company to deep floor clean my hard wood floors and concrete basement floor to celebrate being in my house for 17 years

h.   after floor cleaning, grace for patience in reconnecting my TV (a BIG DEAL because I did not have a temper tantrum dealing with the technology)

i.   new stove and refrigerator delivered

GOD'S TEACHING LESSONS: humility, thankfulness, gratitude, acceptance, faith, trust, openness and sharing, perseverance, endurance, lightheartedness, patience, gratitude, counsel (supernatural common sense), prudence, family support

TO THE READER: **PONDER:**
- Reminisce over life adventures that have turned from "oh no" to positive endings.
- Who was also in the dance?
- Share the adventure.

____

____

____

____

____

____

____

____

____

____

____

____

____

PART 6

GOD'S BELOVED PRISONERS AND PAROLEES

I CRIED AND THE MEN MINISTERED

"Leave me all you who do evil; for the Lord has heard my weeping. The Lord has heard my plea; the Lord will accept my prayer. All my foes will retire in confusion, foiled and suddenly confounded."   Psalm 6: 9-11

July 4th weekend was coming up. It would be four days and a perfect time to travel five hours one way, to a correctional facility in Michigan's upper peninsula. Because this was a holiday and typically, a busy visiting time at a prison, I needed to get approval to see four men in one day. In preparation, I communicated by letter several times with the Warden for this special permission. It was granted as long as the visiting room was not crowded. The official permission paper was to be left at the front desk. All I had was a verbal approval. On Friday I left work at five o'clock and started my five-hour drive. It was 10 PM by the time I arrived at my hotel.   It was unfortunate that I had a migraine headache all day. By the time I arrived, very tired, the migraine was raging, and my eyes hurt as well. I went to bed with a cold cloth over my eyes.

Early the next morning I arose, said prayers, and went off to the prison so that I could sign in by 8 AM. I anticipated a long day as most of my visits last at least three hours. Upon arrival, I was left sitting two hours while the officers searched for the permission letter. Even though I was told it was not to be found, I overheard comments indicating someone knew of the approval but decided to ignore this fact.

To keep my anger at a minimum as I waited, I said many rosaries. At 10:00AM I was told the officer in charge for the day would allow me to see the four men, however, I had to be finished by 12:30 PM.

The normal procedure for visiting is to sign in for each prisoner and wait until he comes from his housing unit to the visiting area. After walking through the metal detector, the visitor is patted down. Next, shoes and socks are removed, checked, and then put back on. This scrutiny procedure can change from prison to prison except the metal detector and patting down is at all facilities.

Well, by this time, my headache and eyes were hurting at peak level. Usually each man comes to the visiting area individually. This time the officer had all four men waiting for me inside the waiting room. I looked like a prostitute waiting to see her men!! I hugged each man individually and sat with him for 15-20 minutes. He would leave and the next man came in. We hugged, talked and so forth. During these visits, the tables were turned. As I silently cried, the men ministered to me. I cried because of the unfairness and disregard by the prison staff of the importance of these visits to the men. It is interesting to note that the visiting room was not busy.

This was a time for me to be humble and receive rather than give. This dance with the Most Holy Trinity was completely different than the planned dance. Human actions changed the God event which necessitated changed in the music and steps. The dance was shorter, and the blessings were altered. God's grace and strength in a Dance with Others can be BEAUTIFUL.

P.S. After the weekend was over, I wrote to the Warden, described the visiting situation, not to complain but to let him know what had happened. He responded with an apology and invited me back to visit any time.

INSIGHTS: Any pain or inconvenience can become a blessing. Ministering to one another is a two-way street.

TO THE READER: **PONDER:**
• How have any of your dances with others changed from what
  was originally planned?
• Where have you received from others rather than given?

GOD BECAME MY "SAVINGS ACCOUNT"

"Never, Never, never give up." Winston Churchill

<u>John</u>

Let go and let God is a hard lesson. For me, it's making another crack in my addiction of "need to be not a failure". This is a God story of which I have been ashamed to tell the ending until now.

In the mid 1990's, I had several meetings with the prison officials at one prison in Michigan. The purpose was to plan release for a prisoner into my non-profit parolee program, Rainbow Renewal. The prisoner, John, had Huntington Chorea Disease. It is a degenerative condition of the brain's nerve cells. It effects the person's movements, thinking, processing skills and overall mental health. For John (not real name), this meant he could not think clearly, make rational and safe decisions. As he walked his arms and legs shook; a person observing him might think he was drunk. John also had a strong addiction to cigarettes. Preplanning was especially important because of his need for safe supervised housing and appropriate medications.

Here is how the day of release unfolded. A friend and I drove an hour to the facility. It was December 22, cold and snowy. Upon release, a prisoner friend of John gave him a skimpy short jacket that only went to his waist. He was a thin man, so the cold greatly affected him. The prison gave him pants and a shirt, his cigarettes and his release papers. He also received a $75 check because he was leaving the jurisdiction of the Department of Corrections. Due to having completed his prison sentence, and not being on parole, there were no resources available to him for finding housing and appropriate medication assistance.

If John did not have a sponsor, the prison would have given him a ride to the bus station and a ticket to Detroit, as this was where he lived prior to incarceration. Because of John's disease and his addiction to cigarettes, I believe he would have left the bus the first time it stopped in order to buy cigarettes. He may not have considered the need to get back on the bus. I was very happy to bring him warmer clothes. To make it extra special, they were in Christmas wrapping.

Over the many months of planning I found an open bed space in an Adult Foster Care (AFC) home. This is where he was to have safe supervised housing. Upon arrival at the AFC, we were told that the bed space was no longer available because the man who use to be in that space came back that very morning! Oh no, now what to do!

Next, I took him, as previously planned, to St. Lawrence Mental Health Unit. Yikes, when John heard he would not be allowed to smoke on the unit, he immediately turned around and walked out the door. Because of his addiction to cigarettes he could not even contemplate being somewhere that smoking was not allowed. Huntington Chorea made proper medication ESSENTIAL. He was given no medication at the time of release from prison.

The Holy Spirit came through, as usual, with an inspiration to try the Ingham County Community Mental Health Office. The building was closed so we had to explain our need over the door intercom. We were told that John could not receive services at this County Department of Community Mental Health because he was from the Detroit area. I tried to explain he had been in prison in Branch County and would now be settling in Ingham County. We were still turned away.

At this point, the gentleman who had accompanied me to the prison said we should just let him out of the car. I said that was not going to happen as months of planning had taken place and this was a person who was in need help. I next said, "What would Jesus do?" (Of course, this was years before that phrase became popular.) Jesus told us to "knock and the door shall be opened" (Matthew 7:7) That is what I and the Red Cross did. New plan:

John and I would go to the apartment of my first parolee, Al, I assisted in 1990. Before that, however, I took him to my bank and cashed his check so he would have money for his cigarettes.

Another big problem was this was the beginning of a four-day Christmas holiday weekend for government and community organizations. It was with our gratitude that Al generously opened his apartment up to us and the Red Cross was willing to make calls in order to temporarily solve this housing problem. A representative and I spent two hours on the phone trying to find emergency housing for John. The shelters would not allow him in because he did not have a picture ID. The prison did not give him his prison picture ID. The police office was closed where we could normally have obtained one. The Secretary of State was also closed. In the end, the Red Cross paid for four days and nights at a local hotel. It was a very nice hotel which was a beautiful Christmas present from God and the Red Cross. I spent the four days taking him food and praying he would not burn down the hotel with a dropped cigarette. John enjoyed drinking coffee in the office as he talked with the staff. Christmas was wonderful.

Once the government offices opened, I started the process of assisting him with a picture ID, food stamps and going to the Social Security Office to restart his disability check. A conservator was necessary for him to receive disability. One of Rainbow Renewal's board members applied for conservatorship (handling money). It would be one month before he would receive his first check. I found a hotel that he rented weekly. I used what savings I had to support John until his Social Security money arrived. Several times a week I would deliver food in an ice chest.

After a few weeks, it became apparent that his income would not sustain four weeks of hotel rent. A new plan was needed. My young son stayed every other week with his father. On those weeks I brought John to my home. This was the only time a released prisoner came to my home. These were desperate times and desperate measures were needed. We did this for about eight weeks. John provided laughter in my home whenever he visited. Here are a few examples of some interesting things he did and shows the need for humor, charitable giving and understanding of the whole person. Upon arriving home after work, I found out what John had been doing during the day. On my dining room table all my dishes were placed like this, one on top of the other, glass then saucer, plate, cup at the top of each stacks. Another day I guess he felt like cleaning because on the floor of a closet there were all the cigarette ashes swept in a pile. This is how his brain worked. It all made sense to him. When John watched TV, he would say, "kiss 'um, hug 'um, love 'um" over and over. When it was time to take John back to the hotel, getting him to put his seat belt on was quite a chore. He just didn't want to do it. Of course, rational explanation was hopeless. Patience was the key.

After several months, it was realized that John's money was not enough to keep him in the hotel and my savings were gone. All this time I continually prayed for wisdom and guidance.

There was no agency that would help. My non-profit, Rainbow Renewal, had no funds and no staff. It was me and the Board. John would not cooperate to get an appraisal of medical care. He couldn't understand the need to live in a supervised setting and refused to go. There was no official guardian to make safe choices for him, no agency that would provide services or family to step in and help him. It was a time of shame and sense of failure because I felt I "should" have been able to solve all these issues. I found him a place that rented by the week. In his own way, he was going to be alright. I cried and put him in God's hands.

A few weeks later I received a phone call at work. The police found him trying to cross a busy street. My business card was found among his belongings. Now there was finally help for him.

Agencies got involved and he was sent to Detroit, where he originated. I was given no particulars. I had to let go and let God do His work. I prayed great thanks to God for John's safety and letting me know he was no longer alone.

LESSONS LEARNED: Pride and shame must go and humility must come; never give up; rely on God for what is needed; accept people for who and what they are; grateful for the gifts of generosity, flexibility and laughter. Since helping John, I do not have any anxiety about my savings account. I know my responsibility in doing my part in paying my debts, however, at the same time, I have total trust in God to take care of me. It is a joint effort.

TO THE READER: **PONDER:**
• Think of a time when you had to give up control.
• What feelings did that evoke?
• How did it play out?

JESUS' UNUSUAL TABERNACLE

"As He spoke to me, the Spirit entered into me and set me on my feet, and I heard the One who was speaking." Ezekiel 2,2

A tabernacle is a secure place where Jesus resides in the form of consecrated bread, called the host. The tabernacle is a gold box located in a prominent place in the Catholic Church. It is imperative that the Host (Jesus) is kept safe. At the Consecration during Mass, the bread is changed (transubstantiated) into Jesus body. In this story, Jesus is in a safe secure prison locker, His unusual tabernacle. There is no telling how many blessings Jesus gave forth during that hour and a half that I was inside the prison. Hence, the story.

12/8/2017 Wake up! First thought!
<u>Me</u>: "Oh it's the Feast of the Immaculate Conception".
<u>Jesus</u>: "Communion to my men".
<u>Me</u>: "Yes, it is Thursday".

I got out of bed and began the Liturgy of the Hours, Office of Readings, as part of my morning prayers. During prayers I thought I will need the large pyx (a gold container in which to carry the host) which has not been used for quite a while. But where is it?

<u>Jesus</u>: "Remember, box on floor".
<u>Me</u>: "Awesome. Thanks Jesus".
I had not opened that box for months but there it was, the pyx in the blue pouch. Excitement was building in me all day for this plan. Thursday night I meet with my group of men in prison. The Holy Spirit, of course, worked out the timing for me to pick up 20 hosts from my church. The pyx is the one I used for 10 years at another prison 2-3 times a month.

Jesus is now in my pocket, close to me. Imagine Jesus being in your pocket. It made me hypersensitive to what I said and what

I did. Jesus is with us all day and night. Jesus is the REAL DEAL! What a blessing!

Well, at 6:15 PM I arrived at the prison and, as usual, completed the needed paperwork (manifest) so it could be signed by the officer in charge for the night. A little later an officer came out and said, "You can't take in food or anything metal." I tried to explain, "this is not food but Communion." Next, the Holy Spirit is front and center! "It's not food, it's Jesus", I said loudly in the lobby where others could hear. WOW! That was from my mouth! I asked if I could explain to the Officer in Charge however, I received the same answer: No.

At this point, I said that I was not there for an argument or anger but peace. I secured Jesus in the locker with my key. By the time I got through the metal detector, was searched, and walked to the school building, tears started to grow into sobs. It was such a disappointment because God wanted the men to receive Him. The devil was trying again to interfere with anger and mean thoughts. WHO WON? Need one ask? GOD, OF COURSE. It was a lesson given to the men that peace is better than fights and negative thoughts. The anticipated Dance changed but was still a beautiful and fulfilling one. We had spiritual communion, sang Marian songs, and prayed the rosary.

On the next day, the Catholic prisoner rep from our group talked to the Chaplain. I sent an "FYI" email to the Chaplain making it clear as to what had happened and that it was not a complaint.

OUTCOME: What could have been a disaster turned out to be an evangelizing moment with long lasting positive outcome such as the Chaplain informing 2nd shift it is permissible for communion to be brought in; two weeks in a row, the desk officer asked questions about the Catholic faith!

TO THE READER: **PONDER:**
• How might my actions and words affect others?
• Have I felt any "nudging" from the Spirit?
• What did I do?
• Share the "dance" story.

PART 7

TRAIN ADVENTURES

TRAIN ADVENTURES

The first train adventure I took that had a big impact on me was November, 1959. I was twelve and we were taking my dad's body from San Antonio, Texas to Hume, Illinois. (See Mini Book 2, "Blessed with Three Vocations") I liked the rolling and rattling, bumps and train whistles. We could walk around which was good for a twitching girl like me. There was no food sold (that I remember) but my mom brought food for us. The train also went through really poor parts of towns.

At one point, we changed trains with the result being my mom, brother, sister and dad being transferred but not our clothes. This created a problem because we had to scurry around and ask our cousins for clothes to wear to the funeral. Then, the morning of the funeral the suitcases arrived. Well at least everything was finally together but we used our cousin's clothes and were very grateful.

My next memorable train trip was to Omaha, Nebraska to visit my maternal grandmother, Mary Sturek. I was 16 and going into the convent in August. She wanted to see me and bought the ticket. It was exiting riding the train by myself. I would go to the upper level and look out over all the land and towns. Thoughts about the pioneers and how they settled the land kept me occupied. On the way to Omaha, I stopped over in Kansas City to visit my mom's sister, Aunt Matilda. She was a happy and fun person. I stayed a few days and walked to Mass every day. I also remember the delicious mint tea made with her homegrown mint.

Overall, it seems like we took many train trips in my youth. My memory is not clear on specifics except for these two trips. Now, in my adulthood, I have begun riding the train several times a year to visit my cousins in Illinois. Each train trip I take to my beloved Hume, Illinois, is a time to be quiet (yes, sometimes I can be quiet!) and a time to observe. Sometimes, I become my sister,

Patricia, who is gregarious and friendly. She talks to people and gets the scoop on their lives. It is not snoopy but is inquisitive and friendly, giving people attention and opportunity to talk about themselves

Three times I rode the train from Michigan to Texas. I am a firm advocate of train travel. Every time I hear train whistles, I get excited, nostalgic and want to jump on. Enjoy the train adventure stories sprinkled throughout my books. There is a lot of opportunity for "dancing with the Trinity" spreading love, help and fun. Think about hopping on a train and have your own dance with others.

DANCE OF THE BROWN SUITCASE

"Whatever you do, put your whole self into it, as if for the Lord and not for men."   Colossians 3:23

"There it is, a bigger suitcase, just what I need". On October 20, 2019 I spotted the "perfect" suitcase to hold all my clothes and miscellaneous items for my trip back home to Michigan. This all happened at a yard sale in Hume, Illinois where I was visiting cousins.

Well, my cousin Doris, had misgivings about my find. Then I found out why. Rather than test an empty suitcase's rolling mechanism and pulling with a side strap, I waited until it was full and time to leave. Oh no, it might have held more, it also weighed more. Rolling the suitcase on the carpet to the front door left me laughing so hard as it kept falling over.

My cousin was rightly concerned as to whether I could load it on and off the train. I assured her there is a train conductor to assist with that need. Sometimes. a person has to have a reality check about "perfect" whatever, especially me! No matter what surface the suitcase rolled over it kept falling. Another cousin, who drove me to the train station, helped guide it but she wasn't available for the walk down the long concrete walkway to door of the train. I had an angel of a lady lean down and help keep it straight. How humbled and thankful I was. Since the train was extra busy that day, there was no conductor to assist loading it up into the train. I lifted and rolled it end over end! Then, another angel came along, and this strong young man lifted it high above the seats for storage.

We pulled into Union Station and the nice man helped get the brown suitcase down. Once again, no conductor and no "red cap" employee to drive me into station where I would wait for the next train. The end result of this fiasco was that the same nice lady came up behind me and helped steer the suitcase from behind as I pulled the front end. No kidding, the corridor next to the tracks was at least a quarter of a mile long. By the time we reached the double doors of the station entrance, I was so flared up with pain I had to sit on my suitcase to rest. It took a long time to recover in order for me to tackle the remaining walk to the next waiting area. To further recover, I treated myself to a Coke and bag of popcorn.

My wait for the train to return me to Jackson, Michigan would be five hours. It felt like luxury to put my feet up, enjoy my snack and people watch. A little later, I spied a nun dressed in a white and blue habit. I walked over to introduce myself and found out she only spoke Spanish. Yea! An opportunity to practice my Spanish. Her destination was Holland, Michigan. We had a delightful chat. When dancing with the Trinity, a person never knows who the next partner will be!

About two hours before departure, I looked up and said, "Bill, Kathy". Unexpectedly, two people I know walked past me. We hugged with smiles and laughter. The Sister came over to where we were sitting and asked me to watch her bags while she ran an errand. I introduced her to my friends. They were also heading to Holland. Thus, the Dance continued, expanding wider.

Time came for me to get in line for boarding my train. Here I go again with the brown suitcase! As it was falling over on the carpet, Kathy helped me and a kind young man carried it to the area where I waited until time to board. Thankfully, there was "red cap" service. I was so relieved. Once boarded, all went good on the last leg of my train dance with the Trinity and all my wonderful companions and angels.

Once I arrived in Jackson, I needed to walk to the parking lot. The now predictable suitcase was protesting, tired and, once again, fell over. It was acting like a tired petulant child, past bedtime. I just tugged and pulled it part way to the parking lot. I retrieved the car, stopped and loaded it and LAUGHED

HEARTEDLY AS I DROVE OFF TO HOME.

LESSONS LEARNED: WHAT AN ADVENTUROUS DANCE! Be aware, be alert, be open to unexpected dance partners.

TO THE READER: **PONDER** on a Dance situation seeing how it intertwines with others.

____

____

____

____

____

____

____

____

____

____

____

____

____

____

____

____

____

____

____

____

____

____

____

____

CHICAGO UNION STATION

"Stay sober and alert." 1 Peter 5:8

February 28, 2018
Boy, Oh Boy! I knew I would meet fun people as well as someone to watch my bags while I went off to the bathroom. A lady I met, named Charlotte, rode with me on the Red Cap transportation vehicle from the train into the station. She was friendly, kind and definitely a godly lady. This came through in her action and words.

We saw another lady and wondered if she was hungry; she looked tired. Her name was "April", and she was traveling from Los Angeles to New York, a four-day train journey. April was another splendid child of God! We three did some "sister" talk. It turned out our new friend allowed both of us to share our food bags and buy her something cold to drink. April and I had a good laugh at the new- fangled drink machine. Later, April said to me, "I am going to get a straw. Will you watch my bags?" WALLA!! Don't you know I had straws in my bag!!!

BENEFITS REAPED: fun meeting new people and God story material for The Dance

TO THE READER: **PONDER:**
Where in my life dance can I befriend and/or assist someone?

____
____
____
____
____
____
____
____
____
____

PART 8

EXPLORATION OF "WHO AM I"

I ENCOURAGE EVERYONE TO WRITE THEIR "RESUME" ON WHAT EVER TOPIC IS IMPORTANT TO THEM. I chose "spritiual" because it reinforced, for me, that I do have training and knowledge in this area. I also created it in case I needed to "prove" myself to others. As I ponder and talk to others, I realize how my life experiences have contributed to my strong relationship with God. I find myself having a greater thirst for knowledge and understanding. <u>Enjoy your journey as you explore yourself.</u>

HOBBIES

GENEOLOGY

CREATIVE PROJECTS

HOMEMAKING

SALES PERSON

PROFESSION

TEACHING

TECHNOLOGY

EBAY

WRITER

BLOGGER

Cathy McAllister, OFS
SPIRITUAL RESUME

TRAINING/EDUCATION

12-16 years   <u>Legion of Mary and Sodality</u>
Prayed rosary on the radio
Visited nursing homes one-on-one
Led rosary before daily mass
Taught migrant children in summer
Worked at rectory on Sunday mornings
Assisted Father by holding lit candles during 6
AM communion service on first Saturdays on the
month to nursing home residents
Made my first Marian Consecration, True Devotion
by St. Louis de Montfort, continuing yearly

16-18 years   <u>Aspirant and Postulant at Incarnate Word
Convent</u>, San Antonio, TX; left due to poor health

1965-1967   Active in <u>St. Henry Cardinal Neuman Club</u>, San
Antonio Jr. College, San Antonio, TX, as a sacristan
for daily Mass

1981   Earned Advanced Catechetical Certificate from
Lansing Diocese

1984 – 2014   Attended yearly Retreat at St. Francis Retreat
Center, DeWitt, MI

Aug 2000   World Youth Day, Rome, Italy, 10-day pilgrimage

2002 – 2004   Formation time period to become a Secular
Franciscan (OFS)

2006   Attended Cursillo Retreat

2015/present   Attending yearly silent retreats

2015-2018	Participated in Called and Gifted Workshop re: spiritual charisms Continued learning via Gamma Sessions
Aug 2015	Received 40 hours training as a Stephen Ministry (SM) Leader
2014–2016	Fr. Michael Gaitely series 10 weeks <u>33 Days to Morning Glory with Consecration to Mary</u> 10 weeks <u>Consoling the Heart of Jesus</u> 10 weeks <u>The One Thing Is Three</u> 10 weeks <u>Wisdom and Works of Mercy</u> 10 weeks <u>33 Days to Merciful Love with Consecration to Merciful Love</u> <u>You Did It to Me</u>

Catholic Book Club

St. Maximilian Kolbe, Mary Magdalene, Entering the Castle, Thomas Merton, Seven Story Mountain, Born Again Catholic, The Greatest Story Ever Told, St. Pope John Paul, II, and others

Enhancing Catholic Books, DVD and Videos

Women in Church History, Rediscovering Catholicism, Mother Angelica, many Franciscan books, Story of the Soul (St. Therese Lisieux, Interior Castle and Way of Perfection (St. Teresa Avila) Total Consecration to Mary (St. Louis de Montfort), Hinds Feet in High Places, Diary of St. Faustina, Four Signs of a Dynamic Catholic, Dialogue of St. Catherine of Siena, Theology of the Body for Beginners; DVD rentals from Catholic Shoppe such as lives of Popes from Pius XII to Pope Francis, "Footsteps of God", series of 10, "Peter and Paul", many saints and others, CD set of 8 of St. Ignatius 30 Days of Spirituality as well as variety of Lighthouse CDs and others

MINISTRIES

1976-2001   <u>Resurrection Church</u>, Lansing, MI
Eucharistic Minister & Coordinator (15 years)
Lector (15 years)
Chair White Elephant Booth (18 years)
Captain for Women's Retreat (12 years)
Youth Minister (5 years)
Prison Ministry (31 years and continuing)
Religious Education Program (40 years)
SEE FACILITATING/TEACHING SECTION

1984-present Donate Blood for Red Cross

1988-present Prison ministry: visiting one on one, working
with parolees to reenter society, conducting
communion services weekly at prison as well as
Catholic Studies at several prisons
SEE FACILITATING/TEACHING SECTION

2001-present <u>St. John the Evangelist</u>, Jackson, MI
Eucharistic Minister
Stephen Ministry
Children's Liturgy
Sacristan Prison Ministry
SEE FACILITATING/TEACHING SECTION

MOVING FORWARD

As one enters into the dance with the most Holy Trinity, a lightness in step will occur. It may start slow, like kindling for fire, however, as this dance, especially with others along the way, momentum builds up and the breeze stirs. This breeze feels like a kiss from God, create an awakening in one's spirit, opening the eyes. Another phenomenon may occur which slows a person down, closing the eyes, savoring the dance, reflecting on where the dance has taken one.

Let us continue our dance, with one's hand in Jesus', possibly reaching and connecting with others. Both can be enriching, comforting, energizing, quieting and strengthening. **It is my hope that these stories will be a catalyst to your adventures, thoughts and HOPE.**

TO THE READER: **PONDER:**
1. What senses were awakened?
2. Did I find I began or utilized my trust in God, in the spirit unseen but felt?
3. What rainbows has God given, during and after the storms or gentle rain of life?

PLEASE, PLEASE, PLEASE HAVE FUN WITH GOD!!!
ENTER INTO THE DANCE. HE IS WAITING.

For more information, please feel free to contact me at either:

contact:	Cathy McAllister, OFS
		Cathy's Connection to Hope

e-mail:		cathymcallister12345@gmail.com

THANK YOU TO THE READERS for allowing me to share my
adventures. THANK YOU for choosing to read Mini Book 2.

ENJOY LIFE AND LOOK FOR THE RAINBOWS AFTER
THE "RAIN".